"Whatever you think you can do or believe you can do, begin it. Action has magic, grace, and power in it."

Johann Wolfgang von Goethe

Oh my Strength,
I watch for You.
Though I may sit in darkness,
You will be my light;
though I have fallen,
I will rise.

Inspired by Ps. 59:9 & Micah 7:8

Burnout's Kryptonite

for the *female* first responder

3 Killer Secrets to Stop Burnout (before burnout stops you)

ANA-CHRISTINA HICKS
Specialist—Simple Resilience Tools
Career Resilience Coach | Speaker | Trainer
www.toolsofhope.com

Photo Credits:

Kryptonite—iStock photo

Author photo, back cover: Barbara Peck

33, 41, 42, 44, 49, 55, 59, 69, 95 photos: Canva.com

Enjoy Enjoy, you gorgeous you

Oh, to thrill in the moment.

To love openly.

To cry with honesty.

To live with eyes of wonder.

To laugh with abandon.

To feel delight in your soul.

This I wish upon you.

Love, joy, patience, peace.

Bless you.

Bless the work of your hands.

Love, *ANA-CHRISTINA*

Welcome!

Whether you are an appreciated, bonafide,
uniformed first responder
who shows up with lights and sirens...

Or a secondary responder like many of my clients—
you are an astonishing helping professional even if
you don't end up <u>at</u> the 911 scene.
(Victim Advocates, D.A. staff, 911 Dispatch,
Counselors, Therapists, Clergy, Ministers,
Volunteers)...

Or an amazing female who takes care of others—
without a uniform, a cool rig, and flashing lights and
sirens (but your life kinda feels like it—and
ya WISH you had some lights and sirens!!)...

It's time to

BUILD
ROCK-SOLID
CONFIDENCE.

UpYourGame
RaiseYourHappy
GetYourLifeBack

High-stress, demanding role? Stuck? Burned out?

I get it. I was… a single mom whose life was reshaped by violence. I needed a change.

I went from burned-out construction manager to happy, healthy, hopeful, and making a difference.

How? That's the beautiful part, isn't it?

Through past traumatic experiences, I met first responders up close. I was fascinated by their resilience in the midst of misery.

Trauma happens.

Stuck happens.

RESILIENCE HAPPENS.

My passion became sharing resilience tools.

· Thousands trained
· Coaching clients across U.S. and Canada
· Dispatchers, EMS, fire, police, victim advocates, executives, managers, consultants, coaches, sales, customer service, counselors, military

Coaching. It's not counselling. It's not week-after-week dredging up past history. It's not airing dirty laundry.

Instead… it's real-life, simple-to-use tools to be able to move forward into the life you REALLY want.

Stuck in the gap between boring and drama?

Stuck with feelings of emptiness and frustration?

Stuck with bad calls, bad days and
increasing stress?

Trade self-doubt for peace and patience.

Trade self-sabotage for joy and love.

Trade stuck for FREEDOM.

Tired? Weary? Broken?

My love for rebuilding means that you'll get **USABLE, SIMPLE** resilience tools to build your **CONFIDENCE** now.

Full of plan and purpose.

Can you imagine?

Burnout's Kryptonite.

3 Instant Resets for the Tired Superhero.

Burnout's Kryptonite, the class, and this book, were both birthed from conversations with hundreds of first responders from across the country.

Over and over, they would share the pain and the triumphs of their jobs. Call after call, responding to emergencies day after day. Seeing, hearing and feeling the misery and pain and loss of others.

When I found out that many first responders (fire, police, EMS, 911 dispatch, victim advocates) have terrible stress statistics, I dearly wanted to help.

I wanted a way to give back. How do you give back to the helpers? I wanted to know their biggest pain points so that we could "kryptonite" them.

We have to identify the pain in order to disable it and start to heal., don't we?

I flew myself to first responder conferences all over the country—as an audience member, not a speaker. I took in as many classes as possible. I talked to as many first responders as I could.

When I asked them about their biggest challenges, they told me.

When I reviewed my notes and conversations, what they REALLY wanted was **quick resets** between bad calls. They said being able to reset quicker would help them deal with the rest.

They told me that an successful reset would allow them to think more clearly, respond more appropriately, and be less stressed overall.

> Results of a quick reset:
> Think more clearly.
> Respond more appropriately.
> Be less stressed overall.

As I looked deeper into hundreds of pages of notes, three themes emerged. They want to be happier. They want to be more successful in their work. They want to get their personal lives back.

So I put together a class that would incorporate instant resets. Burnout's Kryptonite.

UpYourGame
RaiseYourHappy
GetYourLifeBack

I have talked to many professionals who feel called into their line of work, and yet find themselves deeply unhappy because of the stress.

You might not be feeling this now, but have you ever felt like your calling is killing you?

Like:

"I've helped all these people today but I'm dying inside."

I work with many female first responders who are concerned with their health, frustrated with their finances, or struggling with the impact that a demanding career has on their relationships.

Argh. Struggling not only with **bad calls, day after day**, but your own health, money, relationship, family, and self-confidence issues.

And? Let's not forget. Facing real-world issues of being a female in a male-dominated profession can be a real challenge, too.

You wouldn't happen to know anyone with those problems, would you? ;)

I am a resilience coach and speaker. I've had hundreds of great conversations with audience members. Sometimes it's sad. Sometimes triumphant. Sometimes it's super funny. Always, it's interesting.

When I work with first responder or military audiences, they often ask questions about my history.

"Have you been a cop?"
Me, "Nope."
"Are you in fire?"
Me, "Nope."
"You a medic?"
Me, "Nope."
"You dispatch?"
Me, "Nope."
"Military?"
Me, "Nope."
At that point, they ask, "Well, then why {in the h***} are you here then?"

Well, here's what I know. Here is who I am. Here is what I offer you now in the way of hope and encouragement.

First, the stress level shows up differently for each profession. AND—First responders / helping professionals have way higher stress levels than is commonly recognized. Depression, heart attack, estranged families, addiction, divorce, suicidal thoughts, cancer, high blood pressure, PTSD.

I've had dispatchers tell me they'd had mandatory overtime and hadn't had a day off in weeks. Brutal. I've had firefighters tell me how their colleagues go home and never come back. Took their own lives.

I've had EMS folks talk to me about money stress—how they're eating ramen and living with 3 or 4 roommates just to make it work. Medics working crazy overtime to make ends meet. They love their jobs. And it's hard. I've had victim advocates who struggle to keep up with not only the emotion of hearing the trauma, but also increased workload due to shrinking budgets. I've had police tell me about how they don't trust anyone anymore. Depending on how you deal with the stress, it can bleed you dry. You're the one people call on for help. Asking for help can feel impossible.

Almost every single first responder I've spoken to has mentioned that they have lost colleagues to suicide. **Too much loss due to stress. Let's figure this out.**

Here's the deal. I am not here to argue the actual stats for your profession. Sometimes you're doing great. Sometimes you're struggling big-time. The struggle is real. Let's get you some tools to mitigate YOUR own statistics. Your own health issues. Your own relationship and kid issues. Your own self-doubt and fears. It makes sense, doesn't it?

Second, no I haven't been a first responder. Here's the scoop: I have called 911. I have been helped by first responders. They have helped people like me, my family and friends.

And here's what I do have. A passion for female first responders. I have a passion for female professionals who want more.

More love. More peace. More patience. More joy. More LIFE. More More More.

Here's who I am. I am a seed-planter. These tools work when you work them. Instant? Pretty much. AND you need to water and fertilize a bit to keep it going. Simple tools. They work when you work them. So let's plant some seeds and get them going.

I was a woman in the male-dominated construction management world. I escaped domestic violence with my 3 little boys in 1997 and started over with, literally, the clothes on our backs.

Unfortunate truth? **I lived bitter and unforgiving for 7 years after we escaped.** I was mad. So hurt. So bitter. Oh-so-bitter. I was closed off and shut down as a mom. I was an angry, guarded colleague. I hid myself and feelings from my family members. Not proud of that time in my life.

Nope. Not so proud at all.

And yet, we do the best we can do with the tools we have available to us, don't we?

We fight. We get scrappy. We survive day-to-day.

Let's get real.

We don't just want to *survive*.
We want to thrive.
We want to up our game.
We want to be happier.
We want our lives back—without all that baggage.

Got married again 10 years later only to have that
crash and burn after a few years. No violence or
chaos – just nothing. He walked out. Therapy
showed me I had gone from chaos and violence in one
marriage to withdrawal and silence in the second.

THAT WAS IT.

I felt so embarrassed. How utterly ridiculous, I
thought. **The day he walked out, I decided that this
would never happen again.** I would do WHATEVER
IT TOOK to heal.

I was so sick of the patterns. Sick of the self-doubt.
Sick of the heart-ache. Sick of not trusting myself.

Spent time in therapy and other healing modalities
getting things figured out. I wish I'd known then
what I know now. Would have been easier and I
would have healed much more quickly. We hurt.
We learn. We heal. We grow.

I have been a victim. I have been a survivor.
Now I'm a THRIVER.

Be the THRIVER NOW.
Learn now. Heal now. Grow now.
That's right.

After all that, I decided to do something different.

I had since left my corporate construction management job. I started speaking and training.

I've now had the privilege of sharing resilience tools with thousands of first responders. I've also worked with thousands of business professionals that want what I just shared with the first responders!   ;)

This chickadee who (obviously) had had some major relationship baggage in the past has just been married for the FIRST time (even though two sets of divorce papers say otherwise) - because this is the first marriage where I can be myself. What a sheer blessing.

No one yells. No disrespect. No games.
We talk. We laugh. We sometimes puzzle over each other's behavior. We work things out. We compromise. We support each other through the weaknesses. We value each other's strengths. We teach each other. We learn. Then we learn some more. Beauty from ashes.

When you value yourself...

When you value yourself, you aren't guarded. You <u>are </u>still careful.

When you value yourself,
you choose joy.

When you value yourself,
you look peaceful.

When you value yourself,
you stand strong.

When you value yourself,
you sound confident.

When you value yourself,
you feel full.

When you value yourself,
you respond differently.

When you value yourself,
you ask good questions.

When you value yourself,
you set boundaries.

When you value yourself,
you are resourceful.

When you value yourself,
you can laugh and move on.

When you value yourself,
you forgive yourself and are willing to
allow forgiveness.

When you value yourself,
you love and allow real love.

When you value yourself,
it means you can ask for help,
you seek answers, and you pursue
your dreams.

When you value yourself,
you can (finally) live your life.

When you value yourself, you show up in this world differently, don't you? Your stance changes. Your perspective changes. You are treated differently, because you respect yourself. And if things don't change, you know you have options to change things up.

When you value yourself, you'll do what gets you instant resets so that you can move onto the important matters at hand with a clearer heart and mindset.

If you are reading this right now, it means that you are a woman of courage. You fight. You love. You grow.

You are looking for tools to help yourself and others. You are listening for the next revelation of truth in your life. You are working to build self-trust and confidence. And you're willing to pass it on.

During this class, I had an audience member once ask me, "Isn't this just triage?"

Me: "Great question. Could be. And isn't triage amazing? We get to stop the bleeding and figure out the next step so we don't bleed out. … If we cut our hand and need a bandaid or a bandage to stop the bleeding long enough to get to the E.R. or Urgent Care, that's a good thing, isn't it?"

The cool thing about these tools is that they stop the bleeding of the stress into other areas of your life.

It gives you time to collect yourself and think straighter, clearer, and more logically. Get the time to look at more options. Get the chance to rest vs. worry. Get breathing space. Lose the drama.

That's powerful, isn't it?

Imagine for a moment – what if you could learn how to reset your own mindset quickly, easily, and **without having to air your dirty laundry?**

What if changing your thoughts, emotions, and behavior was as easy as using an app on your phone or clicking the remote to change the volume?

Burnout's Kryptonite will do that.

What if you could stop your stress cascade in seconds?

What if you could get yourself balanced out quicker?

What if you could do that without feeling weak?

What if you could do that and not feel like you have to prove yourself all the time?

Burnout's Kryptonite will do that.

Real women.
Real tools.
Real Resilience.

Boost your tools. Change your path.
<u>Thank you for who you are.</u>
<u>Thank you for doing what you do.</u>

RaiseYourHappy
UpYourGame
GetYourLifeBack

(p.s. Here's some pics - because sometimes it's just nice to know who is talking to you…) (clock-wise, starting with the spiffy paint respirator.)

PPE (Personal Protective Equipment) is key.
I used it for 4 years as a painting contractor.
I used it during a K-9 demo exercise I got to be part of.
(35# K9 suit. 60# trained canine. Rocket dog. Crazy hard hit.)
I use it on the track (35# of gear, helmet and armor.)

Resilience is PPE for LIVING.
I was honored to train in the main conference room at Andrews Air Force base. This pic was taken at 6:30 am, right before I got to do a 1-day resilience training there. So cool.

Burnout Just Stinks

There is a way to live Radically Resilient. There is a way to Build Rock-Solid Confidence. There is a way to start LIVING your life.

There is a way to be happy and do work that is satisfying. There is a way to put it into perspective – even on the worst days.

Let me know if this is out of line, but do you ever get to the end of your day and think, "I don't know how much longer I can do this."

There is a way to carry the job differently.

Even after bad calls. Even after bad days. Even after you've tried everything else. There are always options. It is possible to thrive in a tough job that uses your gifts and skills and training. And when you are resilient, you will save enough energy to make another choice when it's needed.

This look uncomfortably familiar?

You losing **sleep** over your job?

Are you gaining / losing **weight** from the stress?

Impatient with your family?

Growing **cynical**? Less compassionate?

Is your job negatively impacting your **health**?

Is your job weirdly adding to your **money** stress (even though it should be helping in that area)?

The job hurting your **relationships**?

May I ask? Do you ever feel like the job you love is taking all you have?

No one taught you how to deal with the all the stress, all at once, did they?

How many classes filled with rules, regulations, protocols, math, science and technical specialties did you take?
- VS -
How many classes taught you how to go home to be with your loved ones after 8-24 hours of someone else's worst day?

How many classes taught you to deal with the pain you see or hear daily?

Most of my clients laugh, and say, "Zero" or "None." You haven't gotten the tools.

It's not your fault that you didn't get the training at the beginning, but it's not too late to get effective tools now, regardless of how many years you've been on the job.

Begin again.

Females have all the same job stresses that their male counterparts do – with some additional issues that I hear about pretty consistently within male-dominated fields.

I've talked to hundreds of women in tough professions. There are patterns that come up in the conversations. You are not alone in your doubts and fears.

"Why do I keep doing the same thing over & over?"
"Why can't I seem to get ahead?"
"I don't want to seem weak so I hold it all in."
Fear of not being enough.
Fear of not doing enough.
Fear of never having enough.
Fear of not being worth enough.
Fear of not being accepted.
Fear of failure.
Fear of not being loved.

Fear of never being good enough. Ever.

Enough said.

How about when you add **prejudice and stupid comments** just because you are a female?

I was interviewing a veteran police officer and she told me this story. She shows up at a scene. And this is what she gets.

The victim says: "I want a real cop."
She says, "I am a real cop."

And this happened MULTIPLE times on multiple calls. From victims AND suspects. They wanted a guy. **Not a real cop?   Seriously?**

(F.Y.I. That female cop went onto a 30-year law enforcement career that had her placed not only as one of the first female SWAT commanders, but as Deputy Chief of a large Denver suburb with a population of 500,000+.)   Yes.

It's important to know that others are struggling with some of the same stuff, isn't it? And even more importantly, **that there are women out there making it really work.**

Not sure about you,
but I want
those kinds of tools.

GetYourLifeBack.

Why Simple Rocks
(and how it will work for you)

We want to be solid. We want stable. We want fun.
We want effective, efficient, comfortable.

Just like a table with 4 legs, if one or more are
broken, the table can't be stabilized easily. It's not
solid. And no fun to sit or work at. When I am
coaching professionals, we work with 4 components
of life: Spiritual, Mental, Emotional, and Physical.

SPIRITUAL: This is separate from religion. It has to
do with your foundation, your knowingness of who
you are, your purpose and what you were built for.

MINDSET / MENTAL
You have confident control of your **mindset-resets.**

EMOTIONAL
You have confident control of your **emotional
thermostat.**

PHYSICAL
You have confident control of your **body**. You have
good awareness of your physical stance and
physiology and how they interact with the other
components.

**We are going to address 3 of them in this short
book: Mental, Emotional, Physical.**

Radically Resilient means having confident control of your reset capability.

Reset   Reset   Get Your
Quicker   Better   Life Back

How about when you're burned out and don't have any energy left?   How about when you're super low on sleep, drowning in hopelessness, you look fried and you sound impatient and snarky?

Let's look at Burnout's Kryptonite.

What happens when the bad guy (inevitably) gets a hold of some pesky kryptonite and delivers it (stealth or otherwise) to Superman? He gets weaker, doesn't he? He even starts to die. It kills him off. Kills his energy. Kills his ability to help others. Kills his ability to do his job, to rescue, to be, well, "Super."

> **Burnout does the same thing.**
> **That's right. It kills your "Super."**
> **...and...**
> **Burnout's Kryptonite kills burnout.**

Q: Hey Ana-Christina – What if I think this is all "touchy-feely b.s.?"

A: I'd say I wouldn't blame you. It seems dumb or stupid or too simple, doesn't it? **I mean, if it was this simple, why isn't everyone doing it?**

Well, maybe it's because, what Jeff Olson shares in his amazing book, _The Slight Edge_. It's that it's SO simple that it's just as easy not to do it as it is to do it.

And as far as being touchy-feely? Yeah, I get that. I had a SWAT Lieutenant tell me that his guys were upset about coming to my resilience presentation because they thought it was "touchy-feely bull****."

He told them that unless they were on a call, they needed to be there.

Afterwards, he was in disbelief and said, "Ana-Christina...I can't believe you just did that."

I was gathering my things to leave. Surprised, I turned to him and asked, "Did what?"

"I can't believe you just engaged every one of my guys. Every one of them opened up to you."

Oh. Ok. Cool. Um. Isn't that my job?

And then there's this Colorado Police Chief who emailed me a year later after I spoke at Rocky Mountain Hostage Negotiators. Long story short, he told me he'd been pissed and angry at the session when I was teaching. He had only gone there for the P.O.S.T. credits.

Told me he'd hated every minute of being there. "Work was bad, family was a mess, health was crap. And then I had to go to this training on a blizzardy morning in north Denver to get my credits."

Struggling with three teenagers, his "moody from menopause" wife, his own poor attitude, sobriety from alcohol being replaced by overeating and becoming obese, plus stress from the job.

He told me that after the class, he got some motivation from some things I'd shared. Short story? He ended up in AA, OA, and went to see a "shrink."

Said he pushed through the double doors on the way out of the building after his first therapy session.

And said to himself, **"That was the biggest load of horsesh** I've ever heard."**

Then he laughed. And said, still chuckling, **"And I was the only one talking. Haha**."

He ended by telling me something I still remember, "Ana-Christina, you were a beam in the bridge to my sanity."

If you think this might be bull, and you've heard it all before, I respect that. I have felt the same way. (I mean, how can some simple tools helps so much?)

Then I'd ask you- STRAIGHT UP – Dr. Phil's famous: "So how's that working for you?"
I'm asking seriously.

Is what you're currently doing working? And if not, are you willing to try something different?

Emptiness. Loneliness. Anger. Bitterness. Sadness that won't go away. Discouragement.

Really the question is—do you just know the basics of resilience or are you actually DOING THE BASICS of resilience?

The basics are the basics BECAUSE THEY WORK. The basics are basics because they are SIMPLE. When you lay resilience as the foundation of your life, it means that you can be more successful, be happier, and enjoy your life more.

Building resilience without the basics is like trying to build a house without a foundation.

You can't build a house without a foundation. Everything depends on the foundation. You can't just skip the basic steps and get a good house.

You can't put drywall up until you've got the framing in, your roof on, your hvac, electrical and plumbing roughs in. Or else it's STILL poor quality. You can't paint until almost everything else is complete, can you? It's one of the final steps. You can only get there after the other steps are in place.

They are the basics of construction. And – the experts agree – basics are pretty simple.

Simply said:
If you can't keep your emotions in check...
If you can't keep your thoughts under control...
If your relationships and health are blowing up...
How do you build a great quality life?

Let's get some SIMPLE basics.
Get it. Get it fast. Get it done.

And when you really think about it...If you had a choice between simple and complex...

Wouldn't it be better to try simple first?

Let's get the results with simple tools first. That means that we'll be ready to add other, more complex tools later.

There are some powerful, more complex and sophisticated psychological training programs. Talk therapy, psychotherapy, stress inoculation (Meichenbaum), EMDR, CBT, etc.

Certainly, there are many other tools than the three simple tools in this book. Once you get the basics, you will add even more tools to your toolbox to maintain focus, maximize your performance, and learn how to maintain yourself in spite of the daily stress and trauma you experience.

I'm not sure exactly how this would work in your world, but just for now, wouldn't it be great to be able to instantly get your thoughts and emotions under control? That means that you'll be clearer and more solid to make those important choices so that you can take the steps you've been meaning to take.

That's how you build rock-solid confidence.

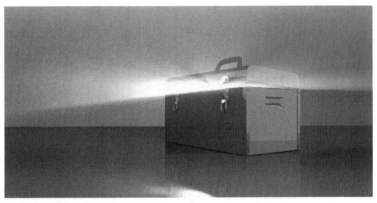

RESET QUICKER regardless of the situation.

These three tools will work, <u>when you use them,</u> because they are scientifically based on how our brains and bodies are designed.

Would you be willing to try some new tools that work—even if they look too simple to work so fast and effectively?

How about if they're a bit strange, **but get results?**

What would it be like to try crazy-SIMPLE tools that help you GetYourLifeBack?

TOOL 1:
MINDSET RESET

Get your thoughts under control FAST.

At the end of the day, we have an incredibly powerful filter in us which will change how we view the world and what happens to us.

That filter is your language.

You know – that little voice in your head that is never quiet?!

 Our unconscious mind is so powerful. It is always listening to the messages we are using. It's crazy, but the language heavily impacts our reality.

Let's check it out. Right now – look around you and **find at least 5 red things in your environment.**

Yup. Just take a second and do it.

Got it? Ok. Now.

Without looking – call out how many YELLOW things are around you right now.

What happened? Did you get all the yellow things?

The problem is that you focus on red, you see red, right? You don't really see the yellow.

Think about it for a moment. What if, for example, instead of simple colors, my filter was focused on the jerks around me. Can you imagine if I go through my day thinking that everyone else is a total loser? Who am I gonna seem to run into all day long, every day?

It's like having mud on your lenses.

Everything's going to look dark and muddy. Nasty. Negative. Dirty. Awful. Less-than.

Or if you have a bunch of fingerprints all over your lenses, everything looks smudgy, doesn't it? And then, it's ESPECIALLY bad at night. When you're tired and your vision is compromised because of the dark, anyway... if you have smudges on your lenses, it makes everything EVEN WORSE.

If I go around thinking, "The only luck I have is bad luck." What will you see the most? Yup. Nothing but bad luck. You get what you focus on. A negative language filter feeds negative thinking. I know this sounds familiar. Negative or positive.

What you focus on grows. The Truth is that you have an absolute POWERHOUSE in your mind.

It's kind of funny, because what we think of as our thinking mind, is really our conscious mind. Our brain is taking care of millions of processes that we are never really aware of.

Our conscious mind works fast. Super fast, actually. It works at about 40 neural impulses per second.

You can't blink that fast, talk that fast or snap that fast.

Here's the thing. Your UNCONSCIOUS mind has to take care of not only what you are thinking about, doing or saying...it takes care of all of those things you NEVER think about—all of the automatic things that happen to keep you alive, storing all of your memories, keeping millions of body processes rolling along...

Your unconscious mind works at 40... MILLION NEURAL IMPULSES PER SECOND.

Not sure if you've ever really considered it, but I'm pretty sure you'd rather have the power of 40 million on your side vs 40?

40 vs. 40,000,000

So here's how it works: when you ask a question, it leaves a gap in your thinking. There is some tension because the unconscious mind is efficient and most often looks for the easiest, closest answers.

Because of that gap, when you ask a question, any question, it creates some tension in your brain until an answer is found.

Once you get an answer, the unconscious mind generally relaxes and goes onto other business.

This gap is important because it means that if you find yourself asking poor quality questions, you're probably getting poor quality answers... and then the unconscious mind moves on.

And when it moves on in this case, you are left with poor quality answers which means you have a poor quality foundation upon which to build your life.

This mindset reset tool gives you a different way to think. It sets you up for a stronger foundation. It helps your body reset quickly.

The chemistry in your body shifts and changes with—believe it or not—your thoughts. When you get a better grasp on your thoughts—your body can calm down more quickly.

Let's talk about questions. You might be asking them out loud. These are EXTERNAL QUESTIONS.

You may not have done this, but I know that, in the past, I focused on a lot of terrible questions – especially in the past when I was in a really tough time in my life.

No one even knew I was thinking that way. These are INTERNAL QUESTIONS.

As we go through this, you will start to become even more aware how many questions you ask each day – some external, as speech, and some internal, as thoughts.

There are three main groups of questions. With varying degrees of quality...

Crappy quality questions:
Why am I so... dumb / fat / stupid / slow / poor?
Why does this always happen to me?
Why don't they ever ____? Why can't I? Why me?

Better quality questions:
How might I look at this differently?
How could I learn from this if I chose to?
What can I do? How else could I look at this?
What else might be happening that I might not know about? <u>What could I learn from this?</u>

Radically Resilient questions:
How will I show up? What will I do?
What other options do I have?
How will I choose to look at this? What story am I making up about this (that might not even be true)?
What assumptions am I making? How will I use this in the future? <u>What will I learn from this?</u>

What do these look like, sound like, and feel like?

Let's start with some Crappy Quality Questions and their crappy quality answers. Then we'll move onto Better Quality Q&A. Then let's get some Radically Resilient, Burnout-Busting examples!

Crappy Quality Questions:

When we ask a crappy question, our unconscious mind (at 40 million neural impulses per second) goes fishing in the crappy quality pool. **Disgusting. Nasty. Putrid. Not a place you want to go fishing.**

Crappy quality questions are blame-focused, think the worst, play victim/martyr, whiny, and generally have a crappy tone.

Mechanics of the question: Usually starts with Why and then focuses on what's wrong. Or who to blame.

- Example 1: I made a mistake.
- Example 2: I am overweight.
- Example 3: He leaves the toilet seat up.

Crappy Quality Q&A: mistake
Q: "Why am I so stupid?"
A: Well—because you don't apply yourself. Because you didn't finish school. Because you are just dumb.

Crappy Quality Q&A: weight
Q: "Why can't I lose weight?"
A: Because you don't have good self-discipline. You never exercise enough. Because you eat like crap. I've tried everything and nothing works. [Notice the victim stance?]

Crappy Quality Q&A: toilet seat
Q: "Why doesn't he ever close the toilet seat?"
A: Because he doesn't care.
Because he can't be bothered.
Because his mother didn't teach him.

Our brain starts to fill in the blanks AFTER it goes to the crappy quality pool for answers.

Not sure about you, but this is not a place I want to be spending my time, my thoughts, my energy, my life.

You may not be sure how to do this yet, but are you interested in knowing how to fish in a better quality pool?

What might happen in your life if you started fishing in a different pool?

Better Quality Questions:

When you use Better Quality Questions, you take more accountability, you don't blame, you are solution-focused, look for options, get curious, and generally chill out.

Mechanics of the Question: Starts with How or What. Focus on potential options, choices, solutions. Assumes control that you have vs. trying to control others.

- Example 1: I made a mistake.
- Example 2: I am overweight.
- Example 3: He leaves the toilet seat up.

Better Quality Q&A: mistake
Q: What am I good at?
What could I do to get more training / experience?
How could I get more information on this?
What could I try next time?
A: I am good at figuring things out. I could get a mentor. ˙I could Google or YouTube it. I could think before I act / speak. I could try slowing down.

Better Quality Q&A: weight
Q: What small step could I take toward losing weight and gaining muscle?
How will I make this time different?
What can I do to get some support?
What can I do to eat differently that actually works with my schedule?
A: [How are your answers different now?]

Better Quality Q&A: toilet seat

Q: What could I do differently to give him a reminder?

How might I look at the situation differently?

What's <u>really</u> important to me—and, is this really worth the battle?

How could I put humor into this?

A: [How does this change your answers?]

Your brain starts to fill in the blanks AFTER it goes to the BETTER QUALITY pool for answers.

This is a softer way to ask.

What could I … ?

What might I … ?

What would I do if … ?

How else could I … ?

How else might I … ?

You may not be sure how to do this yet, but are you interested in knowing how to fish in an even better pool?

The more you practice, the more aware you become.

Radically Resilient Questions:
Create a mindset reset
Get your power back.
Look for positive options.
Solution-focused.
Take full accountability for what YOU can control. Are focused on how YOU are going to show up, regardless of the circumstances.

When you choose this filter, it won't necessarily change the situation (although, weirdly, sometimes it seems to happen that way.) AND it will change your perspective, if you let it.

It effectively clears and cleans the crap and dirt off your lens. A lot nicer pool to fish in, isn't it?

Clean the filter = DIFFERENT PERSPECTIVE.

Radically Resilient questions:

- Example 1: I made a mistake.
- Example 2: I am overweight.
- Example 3: He leaves the toilet seat up.

Radically Resilient: mistake
How will I figure this out?
What will I do differently next time?
How will I apply this and change things up?
What other options do I have?
What resources do I have available to me?
What did I learn?

Radically Resilient: weight
What will I put in place to make this plan work?
How will I get support for my new food choices?
What else will I try? Who do I know that has made it work? What did they do?

Radically Resilient: toilet seat
What is really important here?
How will I show it?
How will I choose to behave, even if he doesn't put the seat down?

Answers: [When you ask Radically Resilient questions, you get better, more resilient, answers.]

Ask a better question, get a better answer. Yes!

As you ask better questions, your filters stay cleaner, your resilience foundation gets stronger.

Not thinking that those examples were deep or earth-shattering.

In fact, I know some of these seem trivial—
but how often has a trivial thing been the straw that broke your back?

Because they add up if you let them, don't they?

Asking a better question means knowing you have full, 100% control of how you show up. You stand tall. How you sound: Asking a better question means you get to trade in the piss and moan for a confident tone. How you feel: Asking a better question means you get to trade tired, put-upon, roll-your-eyes for confident resilience.

<u>**ANYTIME.**</u>
<u>**ANYWHERE.**</u>
<u>**ALWAYS.**</u>

If you've gotten this far, and you are still reading, it means you are dedicated to change and growth.

It means that you are resourceful and wanting more from life.

You amazing woman, you.

Thank you for what you do.

TOOL 2:
EMOTIONAL RESET

Get confident control of your emotions now.

This might be way off base, but do you ever have trouble stabilizing your emotions? Snark, tears, anger, venting. One minute you're ok and then next you melt down? Or do you stuff them and then they build up and threaten to drown you?

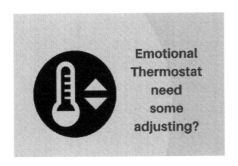

This one is a well-known, but little-explained tool that will work <u>EVERY</u> <u>TIME</u>. It will work because it is based on neuro-physiology.

Let's do some brain science! The amygdala is a small, almond shaped organ in the center of your brain. It is responsible for our fight / flight / freeze reactions, our survival instincts.

The amygdala doesn't have a sense of time – it doesn't know past or future. It is responsible for holding onto memories, especially ones with high emotion or trauma. Why?

Because it needs to be able to react instantaneously if danger is present. It gets signals from your eyes, ears, touch, smell and taste through your brain stem.

It checks its catalog of memories to see if the present situation has happened before. And if it was dangerous in the past, the body goes into threat readiness mode now, in the present.

I know it's weird, but it's like your old memories are encoded and tied to the present. If the trigger gets pressed, it's almost like it's happening right now.

Let's see how we can test this, shall we?

Can you remember something that happened in the past that **REALLY ANGERED YOU?**

Try to think of something at least 10 years ago that upset you or ticked you off royally.

Imagine the details: what were you seeing, what were you hearing, what did you feel? Where were you, who was around, what was your reaction?

If I asked you to think about it, for a few minutes, focus on the details, run through the blow-by-blow, what would start happening? If I had you tell me all about it, visualize every detail and every horrible feeling coursing through your body—what might happen? If you focused on it, could you still get upset about it?

My audience members and coaching clients say yes. They report an agitated feeling, hackles go up, heart rate and breathing change, and they start to feel upset **all over again.**

That is mainly due to an amygdala response. It doesn't know past or future. It starts to send off signals to get ready for fight / flight / or freeze in the present even though the memory happened years ago.

When the amygdala detects a potential threat, it goes on high-alert. The brain gets and sends threat signals, and we dump adrenaline, testosterone, cortisol and a myriad of other hormones and neurotransmitters to get us ready for fight / flight / freeze.

The problem, of course, is staying in that hypervigilant stance as a first responder (or a really stressed out civilian.)

Hypervigilance is linked to high cortisol & high epinephrine levels. High cortisol has been increasingly linked to the following health concerns: (here's the fine print – and this is just a partial list.)

Weight gain (especially around mid-section), sleep problems, fertility issues, hormone imbalance, muscle tension, breathing issues, muscle aches and pains, adrenal fatigue, mood swings, puffy / flushed face, lowered immunity, acne, high blood pressure, increased anxiety, increased urination, changes in libido, irregular period, excessive thirst, higher risk for bone fractures & osteoporosis.

You uncomfortably familiar with any of these?

Because the amygdala doesn't have a sense of time, hypervigilance can happen when thinking about past bad calls, past danger situations, or anything that raises fear and anxiety levels in your thinking. (Like bills, health concerns, family conflict, or fights with your significant other.)

The amygdala gets stuck in the emotion and fires off your acute stress response.

How do we begin to calm down when we feel the anxiety or fear rising up?

How about a tool that is free, available anytime, and gets results?

This tool effectively short-circuits the threat-messages coming from the brain stem and cuts off the anxious instincts of the amygdala.

The tool, simply, is active appreciation. It's the way your brain is built.

You see, when you are **actively** thinking of things to be thankful for, it stops the amygdala from operating properly. Therefore, it halts the escalation of the acute threat response.

Physiologically, the state of active appreciation literally short-circuits the amygdala.

bitterness suffocates in the presence of gratitude.

Ana Christina

That means that when we make the choice to be thankful, grateful, appreciative, we quite literally cannot be afraid at the same exact moment.

BIG IMPORTANT TRUTH: The threat system and the thankful systems cannot fire SIMULTANEOUSLY.

I bet you're curious. The answer is yes. If you continue to throw angry or pissed or scared or nervous thought-fuel on the fire—the anxiety / fear / worry / anger fire <u>will</u> start again.

The secret is to use the tools as often as necessary to combat the acute response. Then you can decide what to do next.

You can simply start being thankful, out loud, for things around you that are good.

But what happens when life is tough and you can't seem to come up with good things right then?

ACTIVE APPRECIATION SCRIPT for tough times.
(Lord knows I need something simple when things are crashing down.)

To be clear, I am NOT saying to be thankful FOR the trauma or the horrible thing that just happened.

I am asking you to find a way to be thankful even if, even though, ,or even when it happened.

It is finding a way to be thankful for something in the midst of the yuch.

We're not denying that the horrible thing happened, so we go ahead and call it out.

Active Appreciation Script
for tough times:

I am thankful / grateful / appreciative

+

even if / even though / even when

+

[the bad or painful thing that is happening.]

Examples:

I am thankful / even if / I don't understand why that happened.

I am grateful / even though / I have no idea how I'm going to pay that bill.

I am thankful / even when / I am hurting and sad.

I appreciate my job / even when / it's tough.

What you focus on grows, so when you focus on the appreciation, your amygdala stops firing like crazy and your stress-response will de-escalate.

One simple and quick reset is the act of thanking.

Q&A:

Q: Do I have to do this out loud?

A: Not necessarily, but many of my clients say that it really helps them focus to do it out loud or write it down. I recommend starting it out loud — for 2 minutes.

Q: Do I have to thank someone?

A: No. This is more of a self-administered tool. It's really for you and reducing your anxiety. You can imagine thanking someone if that is helpful. And — thanking someone out loud will help as well.

Your thoughts calm, and because of this, your emotions will stabilize more quickly.

Q: This short-circuits the fear response. But what happens if I feel afraid or upset again when I stop being appreciative?

A: **What you focus on, grows**.
If you start to focus on the negative or upsetting thoughts again, your focus goes there and you will probably feel your threat response go up again. The cool thing is that you have control over this. You get to choose. You get to work the tool—use as often as necessary. During tough times, you'll be doing a lot of thanking—and your emotions will stabilize within minutes during the active appreciation you're practicing.

Simply decide where you are going to place your focus. Use the tools. Don't give up if it doesn't work right away. Practice, drill on it, and use it when you really need it. Keep going. Keep going. Keep going. You can so do this.

Asking mindset-reset questions, active appreciation, and the third tool will act as a powerful, simple, quick arsenal to combat fear, burnout escalation, and worry.

If you've gotten this far, it means you are dedicated to change and growth.

I am aware.
I am thankful.
I receive this moment's gift.

Even when it's dark, I will seek the Light.
Even when it's silent, I will seek Hope.
Even when it's cold, I will seek the Warmth.
Because...

When I look up, it means I am still in the fight.
When I listen, it means I am willing to grow.
When I feel my heartbeat, it means I am ready to try.

I am aware.
I am thankful.
I receive this moment's gift.

Ana-Christina RadicallyResilient.com

TOOL 3:
PHYSICAL RESET

Get calmer within seconds.

Can you imagine a time where fight/flight/freeze hit you and it wasn't appropriate?

In other words, you felt your stress response spike when it **wasn't** a life or death situation?

Examples?
Worry.
A huge bill you don't know how you're going to pay.
An old memory hits you.
Stress. Anxiety.
Fight with your loved one.
Nasty-gram from a friend.
Seems like there's no way out.
Heated misunderstanding with a loved one.
No sleep.
You just can't problem-solve like you need to.
You feel cornered.
A loved one is in big trouble and you can't help.
High frustration.
Unjust reprimand from your boss.
Humiliation in front of your peers.
Crappy interaction with a patient / client?
The list goes on… and on… and on...

If you can picture a frog or a box, you can reduce fear in seconds.

FYI; Physically, when you have a stress response, you tend to breathe faster and more shallow. These tools reverse that.

It's versatile—Use it BEFORE, DURING, AFTER. This next tool will prepare you for the call, help you during the call, and/or reset you quicker after the call. Or the bad day. Or an expected confrontation. Or a meeting or interview or appointment you're stressed about.

Parasympathetic nervous system:
(rest and digest)
controls homeostasis (state of equilibrium in your body), the body at rest, and your "**rest and digest**" processes. The deep, slow breathing that we do when in deep sleep can trigger this system. Or be triggered BY this system. What that means is that we can control it!

Sympathetic nervous system:
(threat-response)
controls your body's reactions to a perceived threat and is responsible for the **fight/flight/freeze** stress response. Shallow breathing is a result of using this system. The system can also be triggered by fast, shallow breathing. That means we have control over it when we're aware of it.

The next two breathing tools will bring you back into your parasympathetic nervous system which means that either tool will pull you OUT of fight/flight/freeze escalation.

It will help you come back into homeostasis = lower heart rate, slower breathing rate, calmer emotions, lower blood pressure.

It's free. Easy. Quick. Anywhere. Anytime.

If you think about it, **breathing is one of the only systems that we can easily control**. (vs. digestion, hormone dump, neurotransmitter secretion, heartbeat, perspiration, etc.)

What's cool is that it has a significant effect on the chemical / hormonal / neurotransmitter cascades that effect all these other systems!!

> # When you think about it, BREATHING IS ONE OF THE ONLY INTERNAL BODY SYSTEMS THAT WE CAN EASILY CONTROL.

Belly-Box Breathing.

Navy Seals use it.
Marine Corps Snipers use it.
Firefighters use it.
You can use it.

We will practice two techniques now. You can do either or both!!

Marine Corps focuses on the belly breathing (or diaphragmatic breathing.) Belly Breathing. Super-Crazy Simple.

Belly Breathing: Place your hands over your heart to start. Partly to be aware of your heart, and mostly to feel your chest. If your chest heaves and your shoulders are going up… then you're not breathing from your belly.

The trick here is to keep your chest as still as possible, keep your shoulders stable, and breathe by pushing your belly out for the inhale and pulling your abs in for the exhale. Our belly is acting like a pump to bring air in and out. This uses your whole lungs vs. just the top of your lungs which creates shallow breathing—which tends to trigger fight or flight stress.

Chest = No heaving in and out. Stays still.
Shoulders = don't move up. They stay still.
Put your hands flat on your belly and feel it going in and out. This can be easier if you practice laying on your back.

BREATHE IN = BELLY OUT.
Your abs are pushing out, so they create suction on the diaphragm and expand the lungs.

BREATHE OUT = BELLY IN.
As you exhale, pull belly in.
Breathe out as your tighten up your belly.
It squeezes your diaphragm up and pushes air out of your lungs.

Take 10 deep, rich, life-giving belly breaths. When you're serious about getting your life back, you'll practice before you need it, won't you?

Box or Square Breathing
Navy Seals focus on the Box or Square breathing
technique – also called Combat Breathing.

BREATHE IN

1, 2, 3

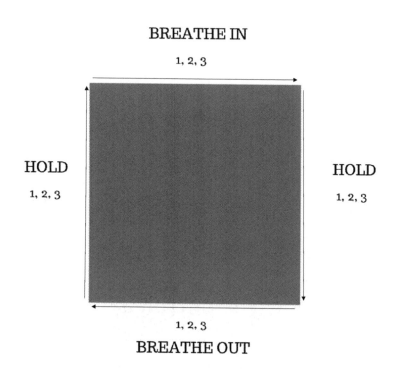

HOLD

1, 2, 3

HOLD

1, 2, 3

1, 2, 3

BREATHE OUT

Seals focus on the Box technique – also called Combat
Breathing. Ric Jorge, Tactical Resiliency Training
expert, teaches both techniques to firefighters across
the nation.

BOX BREATHING AT ITS SIMPLEST.
AND BEST.

Do this in counts of 3.

Breathe in the for count of 3: 1,2,3.
Hold breath for count of 3: 1,2,3.
Breathe out for the count of 3: 1,2,3.
Hold breath for count of 3: 1,2,3.

PHYSICAL PRACTICE:
Start by literally drawing the box in front of you with your index finger. Breathe along with the instructions above as you are tracing the box. Then, after you do that at least 3-5 times, go to imagination.

IMAGINATION PRACTICE:
As you imagine drawing the box in front of you, breathe in across the top, hold on the side, breathe out along the bottom and hold on the other side.

Do this several times and then slow down your count.

It works when you work it.
That's how we are built.

Start with the Belly. Practice several times a day. Practice the Box. Several times a day. Bonus: Do it stealth. Practice your box without drawing it in the air. Practice your Belly while in a conversation.

You know how you do drills for your job?

Not sure how, exactly, this lines up with your job, but isn't this like a drill for your resilience?

**Isn't this basic
anti-burnout protocol?
That's what Burnout's Kryptonite is.**

Imagine what will happen when you practice before you get on scene.

Imagine what will happen when you practice BEFORE YOU GET STRESSED OUT.

Imagine how your relationships will change up when you practice before you get into a fight or "heated discussion." And then USE it DURING the talk.

Imagine how your relationships will shift as you begin to use this even when you realize that you are in the middle of judging, getting snarky, or pissy. They will start to melt away when you breathe intentionally.

Imagine how you will show up differently when you begin to feel those old fears, anxieties and worries.

The truth is that we deal with fear sometimes.
The fear, anxiety and worry don't just die and go
away forever.

Even when you process and deal with the old stuff, if
you're alive, new stuff comes up.

Because these tools are based on how the brain works, it means that they have to work, when you work them.

...which means you can use them anywhere, anytime,
with anyone. And they will work.

Get calmer, faster, now. Yes!

LAUNCH INTO YOUR LIFE

(Photo disclaimer. This pic was a photo of my practice ON THE TARMAC before we took off. I am 3 feet above the ground. No 130 mph prop-driven air blasting my face. No 12,000 foot altitude. No clouds next to me. Just wanted to clarify why I'm smiling and why my skin isn't trying to peel off my cheekbones like in the next picture…)

I kid you not—I used these tools to calm down after an almost-meltdown at 12,500 feet above the earth.

I took an 8-hour class to prepare to skydive for the first time. Solo.

I'd never been "out the door" (Skydiver term. Means I'd never done a tandem jump or anything… I'd never been out the door of a plane. And because I wasn't jumping tandem, it was all on me.) (Actually, I was a bit taken aback when we heard, in our class, that once we jump out of the plane, we are, according to the FAA, a single wing aircraft…) (What?! Sheesh??!!! No pressure…)

Ah, but I digress. Here we are. Right here, right now.

The thing about skydiving?

That first step's a doozie.

I was ok for part of the ascent, but as I focused on that huge hole in the side of the plane, things went sideways. Then I thought about all the things they said could go wrong. Then I wondered if I would remember all the safety procedure. Would I be able to land ok? THEN near-panic hit me FAST AND HARD.

I decided that <u>my butt was not leaving that seat</u> until I'd ridden that plane down to the ground like any self-respecting, logical, normal, have-my-priorities-straight human being.

It didn't matter that I'd just taken a comprehensive 8 hour class.

It didn't matter that the jump was a life-long dream.

Didn't matter that my whole family knew what I was doing that day.

It didn't matter that my best friend and bond, my then-fiancé-now-husband, Wilson, had purchased the jump for me for my 50th birthday.

It didn't matter that I was going to waste over $400.

Nothing mattered other than how supremely frightened I felt and that my brain felt like it was melting down like coconut oil at room temperature inside my cranium. Went into full fight or flight and almost panic-attack. Yup. Ton of bricks on my chest, but heart pounding out through the bricks. Couldn't think. Couldn't think. Couldn't think. Nothing. Nada. NOHOW. Nothing mattered except the huge fear and anxiety battering my senses.

I couldn't think.
I couldn't reason.
My heart was racing.
I was panicking.
I was jumping with two instructors by my side, but sheesh. I'd be by myself once I pulled the chute.

Well THAT THOUGHT didn't help AT ALL when the adrenaline was dumping into my brain and body.

I thought about all the reasons not to jump.

Dozens and dozens of reasons not to jump. Then the expletives inside my head. Crap. Crapalectic. Crappity Crap Crap Crapstorm.

The thing that got me to snap out of it?

I literally thought to myself: ANA-CHRISTINA— WHAT DO YOU TEACH?

Fact: The only time I'd <u>ever felt this degree of panic</u> was the three critical hours when me and my small sons were escaping from that tiny Alaskan island that day over 20 years ago. Our lives were on the line and the panic was almost paralyzing. Fast forward to this plane...

So I thought—What do I teach? If Seals do it. Marine Corps does it. I'm gonna try.

I decided to try to Belly-Box breathe. It didn't work right away.

Truth be told, my brain didn't even work enough to do the Box. Too many numbers (heehee). No, really.

So I started with the Belly.

Once I got the Belly under control, I went to the Box.

Seemed like an eternity before I felt better (was probably 30-45 seconds.) Then I felt better and stopped breathing. Oops. Don't do that.

Started looking at that big gaping door covered with plexiglass, imagining... not good things.

What if I forget my protocols?
What if the chute doesn't open?
What if the reserve gets tangled?
(recognize the crappy quality questions?)

CRAPANDCRAPWHYDIDIEVERSIGNUPFORTHIS?
I freaked out and felt the panic rise again.

So I started again.
Stayed with it.
Focused on the Belly.
Focused on the Box.
Then went all out and did them together.

Wait for it.
Wait for it.
Wait for it.
Ah. There. Relief.

I could think again. And as soon as I could
(amygdala disabled), I started being thankful.

Then I thought about my reason to jump.

Q: **What was I really doing here? What is my end
goal? What is my stance as I approach my life?
Who am I? What do I really want?**

A: I was doing it to expand my comfort zone.

To know that I pushed past a tough spot.

To try something tough I'd never tried before.

To know that I could control the fear **instead** of
letting it control me. That was important.

**It was important for me to do it.
Not for anyone else.
For <u>me</u>.**

<u>So – I fell back on things I'd practiced.</u>

Within approximately two minutes, it was so under control that I started being able to answer my instructor again (we were knee to knee in the tiny plane.)

These techniques worked to the point where I had zero fear launching myself out over northern Colorado at 12,500 feet at about 130 mph.

Amazing. A rush, to be sure, but more than that, an affirmation of pressing into, through and out of the fear and into Peace.

Floating in the sheer hugeness of the sky.

*Looking around and seeing the curvature
of the earth on the horizon.*

*Totally silent except for the rippling
of the canopy above me and
the crisp, clear air against my face.*

Brilliant. Truly brilliant.

Burnout's Kryptonite will do that.

LIVE.
YOUR.
LIFE.

In the end - I appreciate you, more than I can say.

If you read this little book, you are a helper.

I appreciate what you do, day after day.

I am thankful for your skill, your competence, your compassion, and your dedication.

I don't know your story. I don't know how you got here or what you're dealing with. I can only imagine the stuff you've put up with being a female in a largely male-dominated profession.

You are amazing. You kick it. You ROCK.

I know that your patients / clients are emergent when you are helping them. I get that they are hurting, upset, angry or just really messed up.

I also get that you don't get near enough thank-yous. **I thank you.**

On behalf of my parents who got their daughter back. On behalf of my 3 sons who you have helped at various times, in various ways. On behalf of my sisters who got their sister back. Thank you.

NEXT STEP:

This may be a little crazy, but I'm going to ask you to pick one tool (only one for now) and try it for 7 days.

Straight. If you miss a day, keep going. Notice the shifts that are happening as you do this. Which tool are you going to focus on for the next 7 days?

These tools will give you strength, little by little, to do the things you know you need to do.

Getting your head on straight—doing a bit of triage regularly, means that you will have more energy.

These tools will help you make the changes you know you need to make.

GetYourLifeBack.

I'd love to know how it's working for you.

- ANA-CHRISTINA www.toolsofhope.com

The wind beneath my wings.

It's about fierce freedom and relentless hope.

Harness your power.

Choose love.

Get Your Life Back.

We want that – and yet sometimes, it's really hard. Hopelessness and discouragement isn't a sexy topic to talk about. It's not juicy. It's not popular.

I get it. I've been hopeless and discouraged. My sons and I started our lives over many years ago. The pain lasted far too long after we got out. Can be frustrating, for sure.

And it's real. Often, we don't know how to deal with other people's emotions, much less ours. So we don't go there. We mask it.

- With busyness.
- "Everything is awesome and great" pics on social media while our lives are falling apart behind closed doors.
- A drink. And then another… And then…
- A smile and "I'm good – how are you?" even when you're dying inside. Even when you're so empty.

It's not sexy to talk about the deep dark hole that haunts us even though we look, sound, and seem successful. We value holding it all together versus BEING ALL TOGETHER.

Being all together means being whole. It means living with integrity. It means being congruent in your thoughts, feelings, and actions. Integrity means facing the TOUGH so that you can move on with your mind, heart, body, soul and spirit all pulling in the same direction.

Knowing what you truly want is intimately connected to who you truly are.

To get there, you get to choose to admit some things, don't you? Draw them into the light.

> I can't do this alone.
> I wasn't built to do this alone.
> What do I believe in, when all else fails?
> Who do I count on?
> What do I stand on?
> Who do I listen to?
> Who do I look to?
> What do I do that gives me LIFE?

Taking time and space to get really clear on your values, what you want out of your life, and what is most important to you is a first step.

Knowing who you are and what you want?
Now THAT'S SEXY.

Steps to get your wings:

1. Choose to be willing.
2. Decide to let go that which no longer serves.
3. Be thankful for the learnings <u>despite</u> the circumstances.
4. Choose to embrace the joy.

You were built for such a time as this.

You are unique. There has never been anyone just like you. You have a unique and special set of gifts and talents and experiences that no one else can ever bring to bear.

You have hurt. You have suffered. And it's time to heal. Step by step, moment by moment. People do this. It's <u>your</u> time to heal.

WHEN I GET THE LEARNING

When I get the learning,

I can let go the negative emotions.

I am learning.

I am learning how to be.

I am learning how to joy.

I am learning how to peace.

I am learning how to live.

I am being taught...

When I get the learning.

Beloved Daughter

Beloved daughter. Beautiful woman.

Brilliant heart and soul.

*You were built to have peace
in a year of drought and always bear fruit.*

You were built as a stream of living water.

*You were built as a stream of living water for
those you love. For those you serve.*

*You were built for joy. You were built for love.
You were built for peace.
You were built for patience.*

*No matter what has gone before,
you can begin again.*

You are meant to listen. You are meant to create.

You are meant to love. You are meant to lead.

*You are meant to risk.
You are meant to be safe and protected.*

You are meant to focus. You are meant to play.

*You are meant to be curious.
You are meant to trust.*

You live thankful, aware, grounded.

*You are meant to uncover just who you are.
There is a plan for your life.
There is a purpose for your life.*

*Find your wings, my dear.
Use your wings, beloved.*

It's time to FLY.

I Am Woman

Really, for the first time in my life, I am enjoying being me. I am enjoying being a woman. I like the softness. I like the tenderness. I like the nurturing. I like the edge. I like the boldness. I like feeling powerful.

I am gentle and I am crazy-strong.

I am a bunch of things all at once. That used to be confusing. And now, I'm so good with it. Bold and patient. Creative and logical. Action and stillness. Soft and strength. Wild and lovely. Laughter and tears.

I feel. I feel. I feel.
I used to think that emotions were weak.
I know differently now. Instead of letting them control me, I can use and guide my emotions.
I honor my feelings as teachers.
I am transparent in safe situations.

I am peaceful. I am stable.
My Creator lives in me and the creativity helps in the healing. My joy brings light.
My love shows hope.

Rich, gorgeous, brilliant
blessings on your journey.

Love, *ANA-CHRISTINA*

Acknowledgements:

As far as I'm concerned, you can never say thank you enough to those who have truly touched you, taught you, listened through the darkness, laughed and celebrated through the triumph, kept your heart safe, and loved you unconditionally. You can keep trying though...

To my extraordinary support system. You lift me up. You point me in the right direction—up and forward. Always. You encourage me. You allow me to join in on your journey. You make it safe to learn and grow and learn again. To my parents, Gloria and Sal, some of the most selfless and generous hearts I know. I am privileged to be your daughter. To my sisters, Alissa, Tania, Laura, and Teressa. The Varela girls. I love you dearly. A special shout out to my sons—you have helped me be strong. You have my heart— Colin, Nicholas, Christopher and grandson, Marlow. To my special prayer and praise warriors—Jim, Karen, Alicia. Thank you. You lift me when I get tired. You encourage me to shine my light. To my bond and my lighthouse—you not only keep me from banging into the rocks, warning me from running too fast, but you have helped me heal and live from such joy—my Wilson.

To my Lord and my God, my Fortress, my Rock, my Sun and my Shield. I thank You with all I am. May I return to You all that You have given to me. Thank You for the strength, joy, grace and hope.

Always Hope. Eph. 3:19-20. Yes and Amen.

CONTACT

Want more support? Contact me when you're ready for some more tools, ideas, resources. Book your Complimentary Consult Call now. Here's how >>>

Ana-Christina Hicks, Career Resilience Coach
Speaker | Trainer | Author
hope@toolsofhope.com 720-984-1463
WWW.TOOLSOFHOPE.COM
WWW.RADICALLYRESILIENT.COM

Resilience Coach: 1:1 coaching. Call for free consult.

Speaker | Trainer: Yep. I love to work with groups! Clients: Department of Justice U.S. Attorney's Office—SSVAC / US Navy / US Nat'l Guard / Buckley Air Force Base / Rocky Mtn Women in Law Enforcement / Rural Metro (now AMR) / Rocky Mtn Police Chaplains / Rocky Mtn SWAT Negotiators / COVA – Colorado Org for Victim Assistance / NOVA—Nat'l Org Victim Assistance / Davita / Kaiser Permanente,
Book your Complimentary Consult Call.
www.toolsofhope.com

Join us! Interdisciplinary Helping Professional (lots of first responder females) FB group:
Facebook.com/groups/Radically Resilient

Author:

- Tools of Hope: Simple Tools to Restore and Renew
- If I Only Had One Chance to Tell You.
- Seeds of Hope: prayer and scripture cards for the broken, the lost, and the crushed.
- RESILIENCE SECRETS of a 911 Dispatch Professional – with Natalia Duran (interview format – get real tools from a 35-year pro.)
- RESILIENCE SECRETS of a Female Law Enforcement Officer—with Fran Gomez (30 year LEO veteran.)

A very special thank you to
RIC JORGE, Human Software Engineer
Tactical Resiliency Training LLC
"Preparing the Mind for where the body will go"
Email: surfdogs4@yahoo.com

Action has magic,
grace, and
power in it.
Goethe

Though I may sit in darkness,
You will be my light;
though I have fallen,
I will rise.
Inspired by Micah 7:8

Because you got to the end of the book, it means you ARE dedicated to taking ACTION. And taking action means that you are dedicated to change and **growth**.
Congratulations. You rock.

Thank you for what you do.

44760945R00060

Made in the USA
San Bernardino, CA
24 July 2019